THE SPIRIT OF

THE SPIRIT OF HOPE

REV. LUISA DONG

LJ THE MEDIUM

Text Cristina Moracho, on behalf of Story Terrace

Design Adeline Media, London

First print May 2019

DEDICATION

This book is dedicated to Billy, Chip, my parents Franca and Tom, God and Spirit.

CONTENTS

1. A GIFTED CHILD   9

2. A LOVE STORY   15

3. EVERYTHING CHANGES IN
   AN INSTANT   21

4. THE FIRST SURGERY   27

5. AMIDST SUFFERING, A
   SPIRITUAL JOURNEY BEGINS   33

6. A THWARTED RECOVERY   47

7. KIDNEY SISTERS   55

8. A NEW BEGINNING   69

ACKNOWLEDGEMENTS   81

1

A GIFTED CHILD

When I was 21, my cousin was visiting from Italy, and we were traveling from New York City to Washington, D.C. As we were waiting to board the Greyhound bus, I was gripped by the intense need to hear my grandmother's voice. The timing was inconvenient, but I had learned over the years to listen to these intuitions of mine. I responded to the urge immediately and borrowed my cousin's phone card, which I needed to call my grandmother in Italy. I dialed my cell phone and was delighted to hear her voice when she answered, across an ocean and thousands of miles away. Despite the distance between us, we had always been close; I'm even named after her. That day, we had a brief and pleasant chat, talked about the possibility of my next visit to Italy, and said that we missed each other. It was relatively innocuous, the kind of conversation that might have otherwise been forgotten quickly. But as it turned out, I would cherish that brief chat forever.

On the bus back from D.C., I struck up a conversation with the man sitting next to me. He was struggling to deal with the recent loss of his grandmother. I expressed my condolences and mentioned how blessed I was to still have all four of my grandparents. When I got home, however, my family was waiting with the news that my grandmother had passed away. At first, I didn't believe it—I had just spoken to her, and she had been absolutely fine. Better than fine; she had been *healthy*. I got angry—what kind of cruel prank was my family playing, telling me that Grandma was dead?

Gradually, it sank in that this wasn't a twisted practical joke. My beloved grandmother had departed this life. It was an unexpected passing, but at least I'd had that final phone call with her. I'd heard her voice one last time. I was devastated, believing that I would never be in her angelic presence or feel her healing hands again. As it turned out, that wasn't entirely true. A few years later, while I was recovering from a minor surgery in my parents' den, I had the strong sensation that my grandmother was there and covering me with a blanket. She still finds a way to reach out to me. Our powerful bond did not die when she did.

I was born in Italy but moved to the States when I was nine months old. I grew up in Westbury, New York as a middle child with two older brothers, Tony and Frank, and one younger brother, Tommy. My father came to this country with twelve dollars in his pocket and worked hard to make a good life for us. My mother worked equally hard. She was an incredible cook who kept an immaculate home and took care with her four children. We traveled back to Italy frequently to visit family, and my childhood on Long Island was in some ways completely normal—water balloon fights and games of tag with the kids in the neighborhood, going to the mall with my mother, clashing with my brothers, and struggling with being the only girl.

In other ways, though, my childhood was anything but typical. I always felt different, like an old soul. I never felt like I was alone. At night, I often couldn't sleep, and during those long hours while I was plagued by insomnia, I had visions that I didn't understand—like movies playing out in my mind's eye—filled with people I didn't recognize or symbols whose significance eluded me. During the day, I alienated my peers with questions such as, "What do you think happens when we die? Where do we go?" I was anxious about all these feelings I had that I couldn't explain, and my body also responded to the ailments of those around me: if I sat next to someone with a stomach ache, then my own belly would twist into knots. I also knew things would happen before they did. Being around the elderly made me uneasy; I didn't understand why then, but now I realize that I sensed their proximity to death strongly enough to feel troubled in their presence.

These kinds of feelings and experiences weren't entirely without precedent in my family. My father is also an intuitive. He's an old soul who has had his own experiences, even though he's somewhat of a skeptic. Grandma Luisa had an angelic presence. She's definitely an angel on the other side now, but even when she was alive, I believe she was an angel. She was a healer, praying over people when they weren't well. When she put her hands on someone, they could feel the healing energy emanating from her. She was loved by everyone who knew her. Maybe if she had lived in the States, if I could have seen her more often when I was growing up, then I would have talked to her about these experiences that I was having, but she lived in Italy, and I only saw her during our bustling family visits.

When my older brother Tony was diagnosed with schizophrenia, it put a great deal of stress on our family. Like many schizophrenics, he self-medicated with illegal drugs. He got into trouble with the police and went to jail and psychiatric hospitals a number of times. Knowing that my older brother's experience with hallucinations and periodic detachment from reality had sent his life into such a painful downward spiral, I was terrified that I would also be labeled as "crazy." I decided that whatever it was that I had, I didn't want it. I suppressed my gifts and did my best to ignore the dreams and visions I'd experienced all my life. Unfortunately, this did little to lessen my constant anxiety. As a teenager, I went to therapy and was prescribed antidepressants, but I couldn't tell any doctor about the real source of my fears.

Believe you can and you will

I know Heaven must be beautiful because it has you in it. I miss you Nonna.

2

A LOVE STORY

Shortly after losing my grandmother, I met Billy. Even though it was my neighbor who introduced us, I know it was actually my grandmother who sent him to me. I wasn't looking for anything serious at the time, but we fell in love anyway and dated for several years. From the beginning, I've called him "my angel." He was a divine gift from the other angel I had known in my life. His mother always said I saved his life, because he had been acting a little bit wild before we met.

Billy proposed to me a couple of days before my 26th birthday, and we got married a year later. Both of our families are very traditional. Billy's father is Chinese, and his mother is Irish, among other things. I lived at home with my parents until I was married. Billy and I never had a single sleepover before the wedding, and when we got married, our house was still under construction, so the very first time we were able to spend the night together, it was actually at his parents' house.

When we got married, I was working as a surgical technologist, basically providing another sterile pair of hands for the surgeon in the operating room. I loved being in the OR and seeing all sorts of interesting things. Back then, I wasn't squeamish at all, and nothing I saw in surgery bothered me. I've seen blood and guts and brains, I've held toes in my hands, and I was never fazed by any of it. If anything, the hard part for me was not knowing what happened to the patients after their surgeries. If anything, I was too compassionate, too caring. Now, after all my surgeries, I can't stand the sight of blood. I loved that job, but I could never do it now.

Billy was working at Target and earning an accounting degree. He worked days, and I worked nights, so even after we were married, we didn't fall immediately into a domestic routine where we woke up together every morning. Still, I know he had certain expectations about what he would be getting in terms of a traditional, Italian wife. He thought he was marrying someone who would cook and clean and give him babies, and I would have done all of that if I could have. My injury changed everything, however, and for the first few years of our marriage, those traditional roles were reversed, with him taking care of me on every conceivable level.

Billy and I bought our house before our honeymoon, but when we left, it was still under construction. My father, who has his own business as a contractor, was finishing up the last touches on our house while we were away. The first few days we were back, there wasn't even water in the house. We were still showering at our parents'. But I loved that house. I had great plans for it, and I was looking forward to decorating it.

There was a sun-filled room right next to the master bedroom that was just perfect for a nursery.

I promise to love you all the days of my life.

Us in a nutshell.

I vow to support you, push you, inspire you, and, above all, love you, for better or worse, in sickness and health, for richer or poorer, as long as we both shall live.

3

EVERYTHING CHANGES
IN AN INSTANT

I was working nights at a trauma center. At night in the hospital, I never knew what kinds of cases would come rolling in, because we saw everything from car accidents and electrocutions to stabbings and severe burns. The trauma center could be a very chaotic place, and at night, we were usually short-staffed, but I enjoyed the fast pace. It was certainly never boring. My shift started at 11:00 p.m., and I lived on coffee and cigarettes. The night of my injury was no different. I arrived with my extra-large coffee and had a smoke before my shift.

Part of the job was prepping different operating rooms so that they'd be ready to go. That night, I was lifting a series of instrument trays that felt especially heavy to me, and my intuition must have kicked in, because I went to one of the nurses working and told her that the equipment was too heavy for me to lift by myself. She told me, essentially, that I didn't have a choice. I had to get it done on my own. The trays could weigh anywhere from 25 to 50 pounds, and I had to move about ten of them. I felt a small twinge in my back, but I kept going, not thinking much of it. Moving this equipment was just a necessary part of my routine.

And then, it happened. Suddenly, I felt something give inside my back—a strange crunching sensation followed by enormous, overwhelming, incapacitating pain radiating throughout my entire back. I knew something was terribly wrong. This was not normal, not something I could just shake off, and the tears came instantly. Somehow, I made it to the locker room—I still don't remember how—and as I was trying to explain to a coworker just how bad the pain was, a car accident came into the trauma center, and I heard my name being paged over the loudspeaker. I knew there was no way that I could stand in an OR and do my job, so I explained to a supervisor that I'd hurt my back, badly, and there was no way I could push through this pain. My supervisor sent me to the ER, but I don't remember any tests being done that night. They just gave me some Percocet, and Billy came to pick me up. That was my last day of work. After that, I was completely out of commission. I was never able to go back to the job I had loved so much. I didn't realize it that night, but my career as a surgical technologist was over.

The days and weeks after the injury were a blur of pain and appointments with different doctors and surgeons as we struggled to figure out exactly what was wrong and how it could be treated. I couldn't stand up straight. I listed at a 45-degree angle, and I couldn't put any weight on my right

THE SPIRIT OF HOPE

foot. Sitting was impossible; I could only lie down. Even in the car, I had to recline my seat all the way. All the rides to the different doctors were unbearable. Once I arrived at a doctor's office, I would have to lie completely flat again. Sitting up hurt so much that it made me nauseous. For the next year, if I wasn't at the doctor's office, then I was lying in my bed.

All the doctors told me different things. The first doctor I saw told me I would need spinal surgery, and I found the very thought terrifying, because I've seen spinal surgery: the idea of someone doing all that drilling and hammering into me was unthinkable. I remember assisting in my first spinal surgery and cringing then, almost as if I were having a premonition. Another doctor told me my injury could be treated with physical therapy, but after three or four appointments with him, it became clear that he wasn't doing anything that was improving my situation. Eventually, I was diagnosed with fractured vertebrae and herniated discs. Doctors tried treating me with epidurals and Percocet, but that was more about managing the pain than it was about fixing the problem. In addition to the issues with my back, I also had drop foot, so I couldn't stand or walk properly. I had to get around by wheelchair, and I carried a garbage can on my lap, because the pain was so intense that it made me physically sick.

That July, during the awful time between my initial injury and the first spinal surgery, Billy and I adopted our dog, Chip. In some ways, it was a terrible time to get a dog, because I was completely unable to take care of him. I couldn't take him for a walk. I couldn't even open the sliding door into our backyard, because it was too heavy. In the mornings, my mom would come take care of me after Billy went to work, and she would have to clean the dog poop that was all over the floor. Still, having Chip as my companion during those long, painful days was a rare bright spot in the relentless darkness. In addition to the excruciating physical pain, I struggled with depression and anxiety—afraid I would never be able to walk again, that I would be confined to a wheelchair indefinitely.

At first, I hoped I would get better and be able to go back to my job, but it soon became clear that my career in the OR was over. Only weeks before, Billy and I had been honeymooning in Italy and Paris: we were newlyweds with our whole lives ahead of us, and we were looking forward to moving into our new home and finally being able to cohabitate after years of living separately while we dated. Billy came from a family where everything was done for him, and he thought he was getting an Italian wife who would cook Italian food and clean; this wasn't what he was expecting. He didn't even know how to do laundry. Now, Billy was my caretaker, and the only activity we could share, when I wasn't in a narcotic-fueled sleep, was lying in bed watching Netflix. I thought my life was over.

Billy went from being pampered to doing all the food shopping, cooking, and cleaning. He changed jobs, because he was now our sole breadwinner, and put his recently-earned accounting degree to work. We rented out the second floor of our house for extra income. We missed out on a lot of things;

we had to turn down every invitation. Friends would come over to visit, but I was confined to my bed and usually in a medicated haze to dull the pain. Fortunately, my parents lived nearby and came around constantly. They were a tremendous source of help and support.

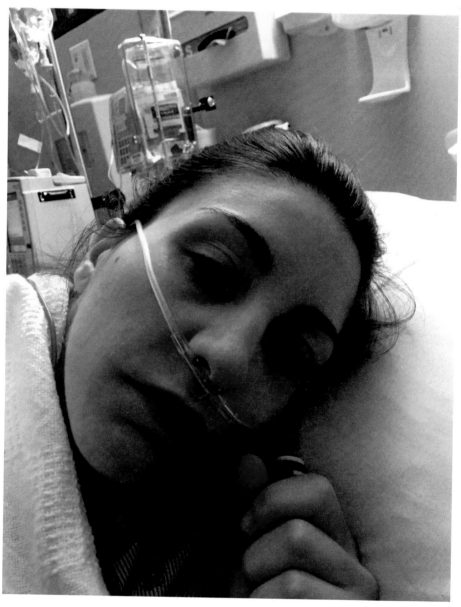

Dazed and Confused
You are strong enough to face it all even if it doesn't feel like it right now.

4

THE FIRST SURGERY

Three months after the initial injury, I saw two surgeons on the same day. The first simply sent me home with more pain pills. The second told me I needed spinal surgery right away, or I would risk further injury, possibly even paralysis. Within 24 hours, I was on the operating table so they could slice me open and install the hardware necessary to repair my damaged spine. I don't remember much from that first surgery, just being sedated and going into the operating room. It was so strange being wheeled into the OR and seeing the person standing where I used to stand. It was an eerie feeling being the patient, almost like a dream. When I woke up, though, I knew something was wrong. The nurses told me I simply had to adjust to having the screws and other hardware in my body, but I just knew this surgery had not solved my problem.

I did not want to get out of bed, and when the nurses lifted me up, I'd scream in pain. I was in so much pain that physical therapy was out of the question. The therapist would barely touch me, and already, I would be screaming in agony. I was afraid I was scaring the other patients, but I couldn't stop myself. Eventually, when I could walk again, it felt like I was walking on several inches of sand, and my back was still a constant source of agony. After a week in the hospital, I was back at home, bedridden again, and within two weeks, I had terrible pain in my leg. The back surgery had been a failure, but it would be a year until I had another operation to correct it. I was back to square one, and my hopes that the surgery would give me my life back were dashed.

The days were monotonous and filled with discomfort. I couldn't get out of bed on my own, so before Billy left for work in the mornings, he would take me to the bathroom and then put me back to bed, where I would lay staring at the walls or ceiling, unable to even turn over by myself. A couple of hours later, my mom would arrive and help me to the bathroom again. She would bring me coffee and a croissant and try to get me to eat something. I had absolutely no appetite. To this day, the taste of pumpkin spice lattes from Dunkin' Donuts reminds me of that fall after my first surgery. Everyone who visited brought junk food and tried to feed me, but I was never hungry.

I was so angry that this had happened to me. I became another person, moody and bitter. I lashed out at Billy frequently: throwing tantrums and having meltdowns where I yelled and threw things. Sometimes, it was just the remote control. Other times, I smashed picture frames until the floor glittered with broken glass. I didn't deserve what was happening to me, and the unfairness of it all filled me with uncontrollable rage.

We started looking for another surgeon, this time in New York City. I had all sorts of injections and procedures, so many that all the nurses knew my name, how I took my coffee, and that I liked to wake up to Lorna Doone cookies. Unfortunately, these frequent efforts to alleviate my suffering rarely did anything more than give me a day or two of slight respite. I couldn't sleep at night, and the constant sleep deprivation took its toll on my already precarious mental health, making me feel like I was going crazy. All these treatments did nothing to address the source of the problem. What I needed was another operation. However, doctors were reluctant to operate again so soon after the first surgery, and I struggled to get approval from workmen's compensation, which demanded I jump through an elaborate series of hoops to prove that more surgery was necessary.

Finally, I saw another doctor who was willing to perform my second spinal surgery. He told me he couldn't promise me anything, but I was ready for something to change. I needed something to change. I would have tried anything. The pain management doctors I saw prescribed me an elaborate cocktail of pills to combat the anxiety, insomnia, and crippling pain that kept me bedridden. I was taking Xanax, soma, and increasingly strong pain medication—I had gone from Percocet to OxyContin to morphine. The orange bottles littered my nightstand until it looked like a pharmacy. Depression had its powerful hold on me. I knew that I could take all those pills at once, and the pain would be over forever. I would go someplace where the pain couldn't reach me. Finally, I told my husband that he had to hold onto my pain pills and dole them out to me as needed.

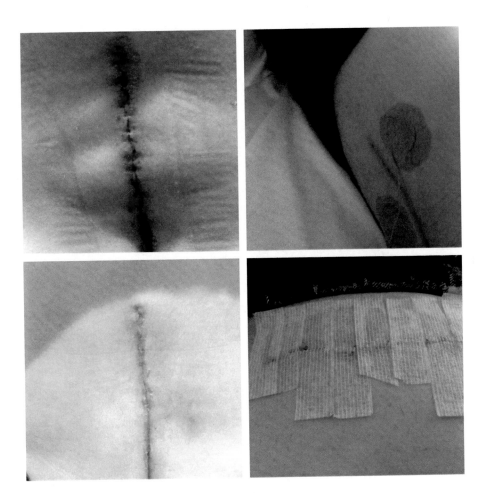

The first of many...
Keep going. Today you are one step closer than you were yesterday.

Chip rescued me.

Chip waiting for mommy at the doctor. Even he's tired of waiting.

5

AMIDST SUFFERING, A SPIRITUAL JOURNEY BEGINS

Before my second surgery, I called a psychic, Bobbi Allison, for a reading. I wanted someone to tell me that things were going to get better, that the second surgery would succeed, and the pain would finally stop. Bobbi brought Spirit through and picked up on me, asking, "Who's in a wheelchair?" She told me, "Don't worry, everything's going to be okay." She reassured me that my future was bright, and then she really surprised me, going on to tell me that I was actually psychic, myself.

"One day," she said, "you're going to be doing what I do, giving readings from your house."

I found her reassurance comforting, but I was easily able to dismiss the idea that I would ever be giving readings. When I was a child, I *had* thought I was psychic, but I repressed all of those gifts a long time ago. I didn't know it then, but that reading with Bobbi was the first in a series of serendipitous events that started me on a spiritual path towards becoming a medium.

The second surgery was in September 2014. I was petrified going into the OR. There were wires hooked up to me, all over my body, from my head to my toes. Being in the OR was a painful reminder of the life I used to have. As I signed all the documents and releases, I remembered when I had been the one helping prep the patients, getting them comfortable and trying to set them at ease. I saw the surgical tech standing in the same spot where I used to stand. It was as though I had gone through the looking glass.

The second surgery was even more grueling than the first. They had to make incisions in both the front of my abdomen and my back—flipping me over at some point during the operation and moving my organs out of the way so they could operate on my spine. Before they put me under, the nurses asked me to move my toes, and I couldn't move anything on my right side. I had no feeling from my knee down.

I was in the hospital for a week after the surgery, recovering. I was still in so much pain that I had a morphine pump, but this time, when the nurses asked again, I was able to wiggle my toes. That moment was a crucial flicker of hope, sorely needed, that allowed me to believe I would be able to walk again.

The recovery was grueling. Before I could be released from the hospital, I had to make progress with the walker, so I started by taking little trips to the bathroom and down the hall. It was an important part of the process for me to be mobile, to get back on my feet and start coaxing my body along in the healing process, but I didn't want to get out of bed. I forced myself to move up and down the hallway with the help of the walker, until, finally, I was sent home to continue healing.

After I returned home, my physical therapist would come to the house and show me how to use the various gadgets that would slowly improve my mobility. I worked my way up from wheelchair, to walker, to cane. I had a shower chair, a raised toilet, and other things that made the house slightly more livable, but I still couldn't even bathe myself. For about a month, an aide came to the house to help me shower so that poor Billy didn't have to Nair my legs after a long day at work. Just the thought of lifting my arms to wash my hair was exhausting. My body was weak, tired, and atrophied. I was getting thinner and thinner, eventually losing 70 pounds.

Rehab started in earnest after the second spinal surgery. Some of it happened at home—learning how to turn myself over safely in bed, how to get up and walk to the bathroom, those kinds of basics. My core strength had been completely destroyed, and those trips to the bathroom would totally wear me out, but things did start to look up. I made a goal of getting first to the end of the driveway, and then to the stop sign at the corner with the help of my walker. I could sit up on the couch with the help of a back brace. I had to get out of the house and move around, go to rehab, and eventually go to the gym. That year, 2015, was entirely spent recovering.

After the first surgery, the house had been filled with visitors. We constantly had friends around. The visitors began trailing off with the subsequent surgeries, though. People don't know how to be around that kind of pain, and I was a miserable person who hated the world. Why had this happened to me?

Billy and I couldn't go out. We missed out on parties and weddings. Tired of missing out on everything, we finally did accept an invitation to a party. Billy did my hair—he got really good at doing my blowout—and got me dressed up, but the preparations alone were enough to wear me out. I was still in a wheelchair, which made me incredibly self-conscious. People stared unabashedly at the girl in the wheelchair. When we arrived at the party, Billy helped me out of the car and into my chair. The first people we saw were my cousin and his girlfriend, and instead of hearing the encouragement I needed, my cousin said, "Wow, your life has really turned to shit since you got married." I started crying and lost any desire I'd had to go inside the party. After that, I never wanted to be seen in the wheelchair again, and I refused to be photographed in one. Now I know I shouldn't have been ashamed.

Friends around us kept getting married and started having kids. Nobody wanted to hang around our house. When I was healthy, I had been the entertainer, the kind of person who loved hosting friends and showed up with trays of pasta when somebody passed away. It became very lonely. Nobody wanted to hear that I was still in pain. People don't know what to say. They say insensitive things such as, "Are you going to be in pain forever?"

All of this put an incredible strain on our marriage. Now the sole provider, Billy had to change jobs so that he could earn more money and support us. I'd never had the chance to put my mark on the house and decorate it properly, although that didn't matter quite as much now that we were renting out the second floor for the extra income. My mood swings were still impossible to control, and Billy and I fought constantly over petty and inconsequential things. I felt like such a burden. Things frayed so much that there were times I feared we were headed for divorce, but we went to counseling for about ten months to work on healing the fissures in our marriage. I needed to learn how to communicate. We each had to accept the other's limitations and understand that we were both doing the best that we could. He was working, doing everything at home, and taking care of me; I was suffering and enduring unimaginable pain. It wasn't that I didn't want to shoulder my share of the burden, it was that I physically couldn't, and that can be hard for some people to understand. "Why can't you go out?" "Why can't you come to Christmas?" People really need to dig deep to properly empathize, and that doesn't always come naturally to everyone.

My doctor told me I would need to go to the gym for the rest of my life to keep my spine stabilized. It was crucial that I strengthen my core and rebuild the muscles that had been sliced open during my operation. I started going to the gym and working out frequently, and as I got stronger, I was eventually able to stop using the cane. My body responded to all of the training, and I became fit. I wondered what I wanted to do with my life now, since going back to my old career was out of the question. I even started thinking about becoming a personal trainer, finding clients like me who were recovering from surgeries and helping them regain their strength. I liked the idea of putting to use the compassion that had been considered a liability in my former profession.

Just as my hard work was paying off, and I was feeling stronger every day, the pain returned, this time in my lower back and my hip. It was intense enough that soon, I was walking with a limp. I underwent another series of injections, but once again, that wasn't going to solve the problem. This time, it was the hardware in my back from the first surgery. I could feel the screws stabbing me when I sat down. Once again, I was coping with debilitating pain. My spinal surgeon told me that I was rejecting the hardware, and it would have to be removed. While he was at it, he said, another surgeon might as well fuse my SI joint, which had been causing the pain in my hip. It was incredibly frustrating that just as I was finally getting healthy and feeling better, the doctors would again cut me open, and I would be forced to endure another grueling recovery.

Around this time, the gifts that I had repressed for so long ago slowly began to reawaken. My older brother Frank brought me my first journal and books about meditation, and he encouraged me to start practicing. In this way, I found inspiration. Meditation became an important tool in helping me learn to control my emotions. I had dreams filled with significant symbols. I tried taking a tarot class, but I couldn't physically sit through the entire session. From the tarot class, though, I learned about the local spiritual center, and once a week, Billy would drop me off there, where I was making new friends—my spiritual family, as I called them. When he saw how much I enjoyed my trips to the spiritual center, he became extremely supportive. As I studied and set out on this spiritual journey, aspects of my early childhood started coming into perspective.

A family friend first told me about Reiki and tarot. She's someone I haven't spoken to since, but I believe that people sometimes drop into your life to point you in the direction where you need to go. A year later, I went to the tarot class, but I couldn't sit through the whole session. Still, through that, I learned about the spiritual center, where I finally found a group of people who could relate to the experiences that had bewildered me my entire life. I stayed in touch with these people even as I was in and out of the hospital. I practiced doing readings with them and discovered my passion for working as a medium.

As I continued learning about Reiki, I spoke with a woman who suggested I come to her ordination. "There's something there for you," she told me. At the ceremony, I found myself having a very emotional response, so I spoke to the reverend in charge and told her I needed to take her class. Billy drove me to her house for an interview, despite the fact that I was in enormous pain. She suggested that I take her class not just to become a minister, but so that I could find healing within myself. I was still struggling with a lot of my anger, so I enrolled in her two-year program to become a minister. I learned about religion and counseling, but most importantly, I had to learn about myself as a person before I could commit to helping others. I went through three surgeries while I was in that class, so many of them were held at my house. The students and teacher would come to my house on Sundays. I also earned my Reiki master's degree.

The third spinal surgery took place in March 2016, and even though I woke up in pain, with a morphine pump, and had to go back to rehab, I bounced back a little quicker this time. The defective hardware had been removed, which was an enormous relief, and some time after the surgery, I was finally weaned off the pain pills. I had been on such heavy doses, and I wanted to learn how to function without them, but I was just like an addict going through withdrawal—throwing up, feeling like things were crawling on me, sweating and chills, all of it.

It was right before the third surgery that I took my first introductory class about mediumship. I showed up with my cane and my pillow to sit on. It was an eight-week class, and the first four weeks were about flexing our psychic muscles, trying to read another person's energy, learning how to receive information, and performing many exercises. The next four weeks were about working as a medium. When the instructor said we were going to bring through Spirit, part of me thought, *Well, maybe I should just leave right now.* The teacher made me her partner for the first exercise, and I surprised myself by bringing through her aunt and making a real connection. I wondered how I was doing this—was I making it up? These classes were an important outlet for me. Not only did they get me out of the house, but I was finally meeting other people I could talk to about the feelings I'd been experiencing my entire life and had spent so many years trying to suppress. One step in this spiritual journey always led to the next, and I had to learn to trust and surrender to this process.

About a year and a half later, a friend suggested I take another mediumship class with her. She even offered to drive me there, since the class was in Northport, and I couldn't drive for that length of time myself. I had taken a long break, because the pain medication made it difficult to do readings. I agreed and took the last open spot in the class, yet another sign of the synchronicity that I was seeing at work more and more in my life. During the first class, the teacher announced that we would be learning something called "platform mediumship." I had no idea what that was, but I was quickly informed that it meant speaking in front of large groups of people, something that had always terrified me. The teacher looked at me and said, "You're a platform medium. This is what you're meant to do." I was dubious.

At the end of the eight-week platform class, there was a charity event where the graduates would be giving readings to the audience. I had another surgery coming up, and I was crushed to learn that I wouldn't be able to participate in the event. Frustrated, I wrote in my journal, asking Spirit that if I were meant to be part of this reading, then I required some kind of intervention to make it possible. At the next class, the teacher informed us there had been a change in the scheduling, and that the event was now happening on a day before my surgery. I was thrilled, but this also meant that I was committed. I would be giving readings in front of a room full of people. It was the first event I participated in where my parents and Billy came to support me and see my gifts in action. I gave two readings that night and did something called a "double link" with my mentor, Winter Brook. I was so emotional that I cried during the readings.

The day I made it down the driveway.
Believe in yourself you are stronger than you think.

For every dark night there's a brighter day.

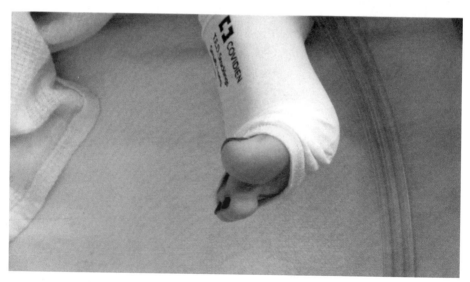

This is the day I received my second chance. The moment of hope.
I woke up from surgery with feeling and able to wiggle my toes!
Miracles happen.

That day the sun was shining a bit brighter. An outing after being indoors
for way too long.

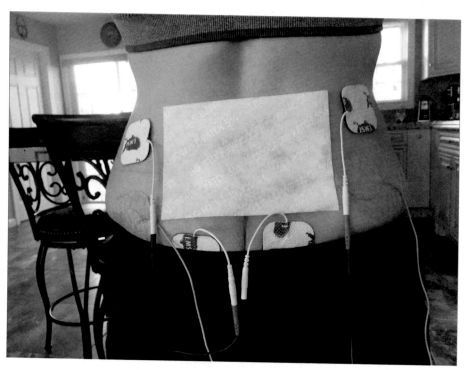

Part of my daily routine. A gadget here and a gadget there.
Anything for some relief.

6

A THWARTED RECOVERY

Around the end of 2016, I started having problems with my stomach: sharp pains and attacks. I kept eating less and less, and I was getting thinner and thinner. In an effort to diagnose the problem, I had an endoscopy and a colonoscopy, but they didn't provide any answers. I had been working out regularly and was even thinking about entering competitions, and I had put down a deposit at Hofstra for their personal trainer program, but my stomach problems soon put an end to all of that. I was on antacids, because the pain pills had destroyed my stomach lining, but every time I ate, I would get sick. I was nauseous and coughing up bile all the time. Just lying down would make me vomit. I was less than 90 pounds at this point, and I told my doctor I knew something wasn't right. Finally, after another series of tests, the doctor told me my small intestine was compressed between my aorta and my superior mesenteric artery. That night, I was sent to the hospital to get ready for my fourth major operation. It was an emergency surgery, and my parents had to fly home from their vacation in Italy to be with me in the hospital.

When they were doing that surgery, they found out I had another rare condition, Nutcracker Syndrome. Because I'd lost so much weight, I had no fat around my organs, and my renal vein was compressed. I had blood in my urine and kidney pain; my kidney couldn't filter out the blood, so it was making new veins. I was afraid of losing the kidney. I was tired, and I'd had enough, and I wouldn't have been surprised if I didn't wake up after the operation. My stomach surgery was in June, and the first kidney surgery was in November, so I had barely recovered from one before it was time to go under the knife again. I fell back into depression, wondering if this series of medical nightmares would ever come to an end. I had to put my new dreams about becoming a personal trainer on hold. I looked anorexic, and gaining weight became a major priority. Billy and my parents brought me many chocolate milkshakes, but I struggled to pack on some of the pounds I'd lost. I was on a liquid diet for a month, and then I moved on to soft foods, and eventually back to solids, but with many restrictions.

On Thanksgiving, while I was in the hospital recovering from the kidney surgery, I was shaking and feverish. I prayed to my grandmother for her to help me, and I calmed down right away and fell asleep. I still see her in my dreams and feel her presence frequently. She's been a huge part of my spiritual journey. Knowing that she's able to still communicate with me opened my mind to the idea that other people's loved ones may be able to make themselves heard.

When I was in the hospital for one of my surgeries, my roommate was visiting with her granddaughter, which made me miss my own grandmother. The pain was intense that day, and I was crying hysterically while I waited for the nurses to administer the next round of my medication. Suddenly, I felt as though someone had gotten in the bed with me and was spooning me while stroking my cheek with their hand. It was such a comforting presence that I immediately fell asleep. The next time I spoke with the nurse, she told me that when she came around to give me my medication, I had seemed so peaceful that she didn't want to disturb me. I slept through that whole night without any pain meds. The next day I spoke to my father, who was visiting family in Italy, and I told him, "I need you to put white flowers on Grandma's grave and tell her thank you." He said, "I can't believe you just said that." He had just left the cemetery, and there had been white flowers on her grave already. To this day, we've never been able to find out who put those flowers there. That was all the confirmation I needed that my grandmother had been with me in the hospital that day.

The first kidney surgery was a failure, and after that operation, the doctor recommended that I have the kidney removed altogether. It was a healthy kidney, and I decided I wanted to donate it—it had to come out anyway, and I thought maybe something good could come of this situation. I was the first Nutcracker patient at that hospital to donate a kidney. They weren't sure it would work, and they told the recipient that, warning her that nothing was guaranteed. By the time I had the second kidney surgery, I was exhausted. I thought maybe this was all for something—maybe I could save a life. My operation was a success, and the transplant was, as well. There were so many people in the OR when I went in, because there were two surgical teams, and I went in crying, worried I wouldn't wake up, and knowing what I would face in terms of a painful recovery.

The best view comes after the hardest climb.

At my second home: New York Spine Institute. Fall six times, get up seven.

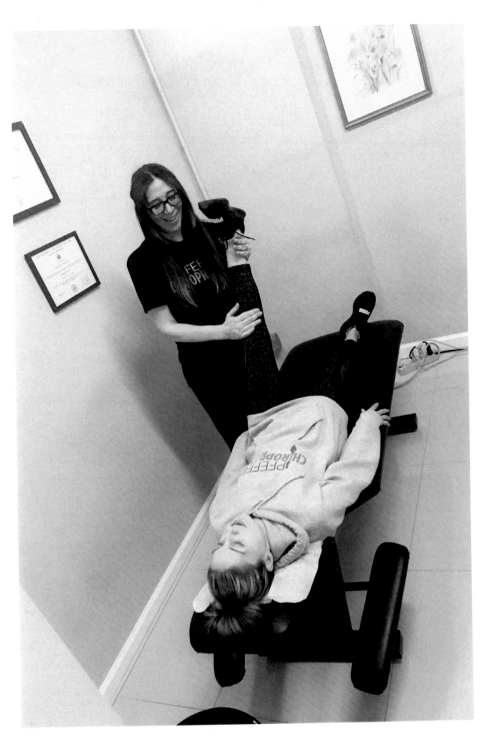

Stretching and massage therapy with Dr. Michelle Pfeffer.

The nurse did my hair after a week in the hospital for emergency SMAS surgery. If at first you don't succeed fix your ponytail and try again.

7

KIDNEY SISTERS

Winter Brook was an amazing mentor to me. She was hugely supportive during my kidney surgery. She came to the hospital and told me my grandmother was right there, at my bedside. She encouraged me during my recovery when I was afraid that my gifts would atrophy from lack of use. All the pain and medication muffled my gifts and made it difficult to perform readings. Having just recently accessed these parts of myself that I had been suppressing since adolescence, I was afraid I would now lose them all over again. Winter Brook reassured me they would not slip away quite so easily. In fact, during a phone call once I was home, as I lamented this potential loss, she suggested I do a reading for her right there, on the spot. I'd never read her before, but I brought through her father, and she told me I had nothing to worry about. Even though I hadn't known Winter Brook for very long, our connection was profound. It felt as though she could have been my mother in another life. When I donated my kidney, she used social media to rally her followers to send me healing from all over the world. As

I began doing more readings, she sent me referrals, got me speaking gigs, and always pushed me to keep going, even when I was worn out from surgeries and wanted to give up. We support each other and share the platform. We recently did a Celebration of Life event to celebrate the one-year anniversary of my kidney removal, and all the funds went to the National Kidney Foundation. She's brought me so many opportunities, and as much as I look up to her, she also says that I inspire her. She introduced me to many friends who have been an important part of my spiritual journey.

All mediums work differently. When I'm working, I call in Spirit, a light being, to help me reach those who have passed over. There's a team of helpers up there who are guiding us to get where we need to go and making everything down here happen. I'm able to see pictures, almost like a flash. There's a screen in my mind's eye, although now I'm able to do it with my eyes open, focused on a blank wall. When I see symbols, I have to interpret them. For example, during one reading, I got a flash of a music note, and it turned out the person was a music teacher. But these symbols are open to interpretation. An apple could mean someone is a teacher, or it could just mean someone loves apples. Spirit is going to give you what's in your frame of reference, but it expands your frame of reference. Sometimes, it's like getting a bad Wifi connection; you're not always getting full, clear sentences. I also hear things—music or individual words—and sometimes, I just know things. I'm human, and I can make mistakes or misinterpret information, but taking classes helped me develop these methods of receiving information and following my own intuition. If you can learn how to tap into that voice, then you can unlock your own psychic abilities. I do believe it can be taught, if the student is willing to learn.

There is a difference between a psychic and a medium. Psychics can tap into your past or see things that are happening now, or maybe three months from now. A medium can do all the things a psychic can do, but they can also connect with loved ones who have passed on. All mediums are psychic, but not all psychics are mediums. See, hear, feel, know—just like any other skill, it requires practice. I practice every day.

When I sit with a client, I explain how I work and ask him or her to have an open mind and an open heart. We can't control who comes through; you might want to talk to Mom, and Dad comes through, instead. Some people make their way to the front of the line. I might bring through someone with whom the client does not want to talk. I once brought through a woman's ex-husband, and her response was, "I don't want to talk to him." Once, I was doing a platform reading, and I brought through a little girl. It turned out she was the daughter of an audience member's friend, a woman who was supposed to be there that night but couldn't make it. She came through so that the woman in the audience could be a messenger.

Every reading is a surprise. Some people want the facts, the evidence (names, birthdays, etc.). They want proof. Other people just want to know that their loved one is at peace. I did a party for a group once on a Monday night after work. From the moment I walked into the room, I could tell that the energy was low, which makes a difference in a reading. On a Friday night, I've noticed the vibration is higher, and the higher the vibration, the better the communication. During the reading, I said to the man that I was seeing a man with a connection to a restaurant, someone who had worked in restaurant. He said "no, no" to everything. At the end of the reading, he told me he believed I had brought through his father. It turned out his father didn't work at a restaurant—he *owned* a restaurant. He missed an opportunity to get a message from his dad. That's why I tell people to keep an open mind. One woman told me, after I brought through her dad, that no one had ever brought through her dad before, and she had been at my event on her birthday because she'd won the ticket in a raffle, and even before she attended, she had been thinking that the ticket was a birthday gift from her father. That synchronicity keeps appearing.

My kidney was donated to a 26-year-old woman, Kelly, from New York who became my "kidney sister." She had been on dialysis since she was eighteen. Her mother had also passed from kidney disease, which ran in her family. The doctors explained to her that they had never transplanted a Nutcracker kidney before, and they weren't 100% positive it would work. I met her the day of the procedure and gave her a gift, a necklace that was part of a matching set. One necklace had a kidney charm in it, and the other had an empty space where the kidney would have been.

Kelly and I even share a physical resemblance that made the experience a little eerie. Living donors don't always choose to meet the recipient, but not only did I meet her, we kept in touch. I was afraid of getting attached to her. If, god forbid, something happened to her, I didn't want to feel responsible. The living donor psych tests are incredibly thorough, and you have to meet with a social worker several times to help negotiate the process. They ask you to consider all sorts of different scenarios that might arise down the line. *What if you found out a family member needed a kidney, but you already gave your kidney away? What if you donated your kidney, and it failed. Would you feel responsible? What if something happens to your remaining kidney, and you need dialysis?* It was a little easier for me, because my kidney had to come out no matter what, but it's still quite an ordeal.

Sometimes Kelly would message me from the hospital, or text me messages like, "Your kidney is slow today," or "I might lose the kidney," and I would take it personally. I would see her on social media and worry that she wasn't taking good enough care of the kidney I had given her. She was out trying to make up for the seven years that she had been tethered to a dialysis machine, but I worried about her. I spoke to my social worker, who recommended I have a break from following her on social media and take a step back. We're still in touch, but I didn't expect to have such a complicated relationship with her. It's a permanent connection. Most people donate to family members, not strangers, so it's an interesting dynamic. We reunited for our one-year kidney anniversary and met for lunch. She looked healthy and happy and is doing so much, traveling the world and applying to graduate school. I'm so thrilled I could give her the opportunity to have such a full life now.

I had heard that the recipient can pick up traits from the donor, but I was still taken aback by just how much that proved to be true with Kelly. She told me that after she received my kidney, she started craving brownies all the time—my favorite dessert. And ever since she's had my kidney, she's been feeling her mom's presence and dreaming of her. She's become an empath and is struggling with feeling other people's emotions. She got a lot more than my kidney.

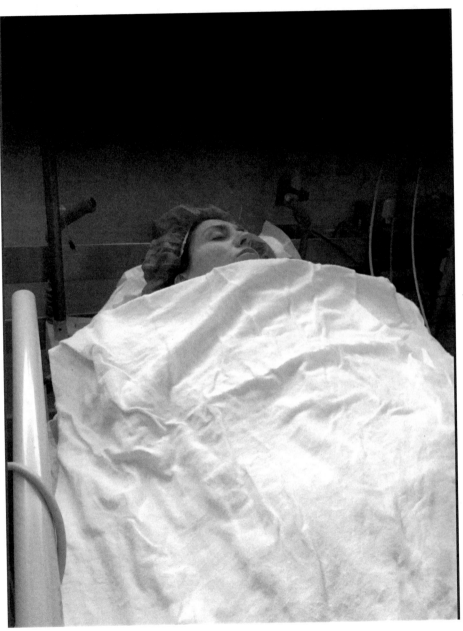

Dreaming of good news. Wake me up when it's all over.

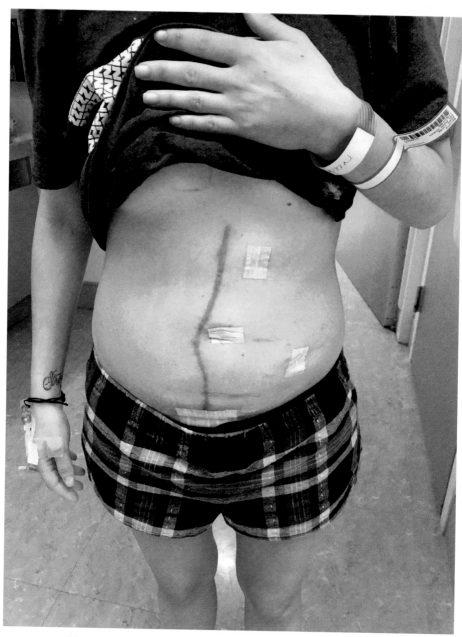

A few more incisions and scars—makes for some interesting stories. I look like The Flash don't you think?

Dreams do come true. First time in Disney with my very own Prince William.

Let the sea set you free. Meditating in Aruba. It really is one happy Island.

One year post-donation blood work! First clean bill of health in six years!

Celebrating life with my mentor, healer, and friend, Winter Brook.

My mom, dad, and Billy on our first family vacation together in Rome.
I would not have made it here if it weren't for these three.
They are my life savers.

8

A NEW BEGINNING

Billy and I celebrated our five-year anniversary in May 2018 and dedicated much of that year to making up for some of the time we'd lost. Now that I was well enough to travel again, I couldn't get enough of it. In July, he surprised me with a trip to Disney World. That September, I traveled to Sedona, Arizona for a spiritual retreat, and in November, we took a vacation in Aruba. We went back to Italy to see my family for New Year's, and we retraced some steps of our honeymoon in Rome. We celebrated everything coming full circle.

I don't miss my old job, even though I miss being able to do it. I'm reaching and helping more people now, and it's so much more fulfilling. Working as a medium is such a powerful experience. Doing a reading gives me a feeling that's almost like a high—*how did I know that? How did I reach that person?* It's an amazing feeling. Billy was skeptical of my medium gifts at first, but now he says I'm right about too much for him not to believe. Things that used to scare me don't anymore. I used to be terrified of heights and deep water, but they no longer inspire the intense fear in me they once did.

As difficult as it was to endure all the physical pain, to have my expectations about my life and career and marriage shattered and rebuilt, this all brought me closer to my parents and to Billy. It's made our marriage stronger. It was hard for my oldest brother to see me this way. There were times when he couldn't come to the hospital, but he's still my big brother. Frank, my middle brother, brought me the spiritual books and books about meditation, so in some ways, he set me on the journey that changed my life forever. I lost a lot of family and friends. Something like this really shows you who is prepared to stick with you when life gets tough. But now I know that the people I have around me are people I can truly count on.

I have clients who are teenage girls experiencing the same sense of alienation I once felt, or they are in possession of gifts they don't even know they have, or they're grappling with massive anxiety, like what I dealt with during my adolescence. Sometimes it's like the universe casts a huge circle around you. Every morning when I wake up, I thank Spirit for this day and ask how I can help others. I'm so grateful to be where I am. I once thought I might not be able to walk again. I feared I would be in a wheelchair for the rest of my life. Now as I embrace my recovery, I ask every day how I can pay it forward.

I look to the future with a genuine sense of excitement. I want to continue growing as a medium so I can reach more people. I want to save money and become financially independent again. I want us to keep traveling, because there was a point in my life when I didn't think I could ever get on another plane. I'll never take that for granted. I'm involved with the National Kidney Foundation, active with support groups, and I want to stay involved with kidney awareness. I want to get back to being fit and going to yoga, being healthy. I'm at a solid, strong starting point, and I just want to grow from here.

Having kids may no longer be in the cards for us, but I gave the miracle of life when I donated my kidney. Billy and I are just happy to enjoy each other, and the room in our house that would have been our nursery is now my office. A pregnancy would just not be physically possible for me. I would need to be on bed rest the entire time, and the changes to my body could distort my spine, putting me at risk for further disability or even death. Billy and I discussed it, and he told me he would rather have me here, alive and with him, than lose me and be left with a child to take care of on his own. I've done that grieving. It is hard sometimes seeing friends who are having kids and knowing that that will never be me. But it's more important to me to feel healthy and strong. There are so many other things that I can do. We never got to have the honeymoon phase of our marriage, and we're still making up for a lot of that lost time.

I'm doing what I'm meant to do. I'm an ordained minister now. I do spiritual counseling, and I perform wedding ceremonies and baby blessings. I also mentor new mediums, helping them learn how to use their gifts. I do monthly healing workshops at my house. Every month is a different topic, whatever Spirit makes me do that day—gratitude, for example. We do a meditation, have a discussion, and at the end, I do spot readings. It's gotten so popular that I had to add another day. Everybody has something they need to heal.

I've been using the name "LJ the Medium." When Billy and I started dating, he called me "LJ," short for Luisa Jennifer. When I got sick, I went off social media, and when I eventually went back on, I used this new moniker, instead. It also became the name by which all my friends in the spiritual community know me, so eventually, I started using it for my professional medium work.

Looking back now, I understand that I needed to go through all of that. I needed to learn compassion, to trust and believe and have faith. I regret losing friends and loved ones. When we're not healthy and not in our proper state of mind, we do or say things that we regret. I regret how I treated some people. I know there were times when I said things that I shouldn't have said, and I regret that I didn't live more prior to my injury, because now there are things I'll never be able to do. There are little things I took for granted. Now, I'm well enough to travel, but I still can't put my own luggage in the overhead compartment. There are certain physical limitations I'll be dealing with for the rest of my life, so I wish I had been more adventurous back when I was capable of zip lining and doing all of those bucket list items we always think we'll have time to do later. I wish I could have learned all of these lessons in a less painful way, but there were lessons that needed to be learned, people who needed to be lost, and I don't regret the changes in my life that have gotten me to the place where I am now. I've mourned for the life I used to have, and I love the life that I have now. My relationships with my parents and Billy are stronger than ever. I have a career that fulfills me and allows me to connect with and help people.

I've recently made other changes to battle the fatigue and anemia that still plague me. I have to limit my protein, salt, and sugar, because my one kidney can only process so much. I've been going to the gym three or four times a week, doing it on my own without a trainer or a physical therapist. I'm exercising and eating healthy, and it's making a huge difference. I still go to massage therapy three times a week. Taking care of myself has to be a priority—mind, body, and soul. I'm a minister, telling people at my workshops how to be healthy, and I need to take my own advice. It's a process though; it doesn't happen overnight. Healing requires patience, no matter how much we want to feel better right now. After not knowing if I'd ever drive again and having to turn in a brand-new car because it sat in the driveway for three years, now I'm back on the road. I'm getting used to being back on the road and can't drive long distances yet, but it's given me back my sense of independence. Even though life is busier, Billy and I still enjoy watching movies, and some our new hobbies include fishing, going to shows, and traveling. I even got to be an extra in a movie, and we went to our first movie premiere. I keep getting calls for additional work, and I'm excited to do more of that in the future. All of this began right after our wedding, and now this book will be coming out around our sixth wedding anniversary, so it will be a great way to celebrate that special occasion.

My parents and Bill have been the source of my strength through all of this. My mom helping me cook and clean when I couldn't get out of bed was an enormous gift. Billy took me to so many doctor appointments, and when he couldn't do it, my dad pitched in. Nothing was easy, but their strength gave me strength, and they supported me when I thought I would never have my health again. After my first spinal surgery, I got the word "strength" tattooed on my wrist. At the time, I was on heavy painkillers, so it didn't hurt at all, and every time I laid down on an operating table or lifted my arm to give blood, I would see that tattoo and remember. The nurses would read it and say, "Yes, you do have strength." I wore strength, and I had strength, and I will continue to do so for the rest of my life.

LJ the Medium

An amazing night sharing my story and giving readings.

LJ the Rev

Six years ago or even just one year ago I would've never pictured my life the way it is now. No matter how hard it gets, someday you will look back and realize your struggles changed your life for the better.

Six years strong.
Loved you then. Love you still. Always have, always will.

ACKNOWLEDGEMENTS

Thanks to Billy—I wouldn't be here if it weren't for him. He is my rock and the glue that held me together. He is truly a blessing, and I'm so grateful he never gave up on me. What we went through made us stronger. He is my best friend, the love of my life, my everything. He was there 24/7. He worked hard to pay the bills, took time off to be in the hospital or take me to appointments, and he spent hours driving me around. He stepped up as a man to take care of me and our household, and in the process, he made many sacrifices and lost a lot of sleep. I'm not the only one who went through this; he did, too. I'm so grateful to him for fighting hard for our marriage, and for loving me and making me feel special even through the darkest times. He supports me completely and believes in everything I do.

Thanks to my parents, who have always believed I could do anything, ever since I was a little girl. They always supported me and showed me what it was to have strength. I wouldn't be where I am today without their love and help. Rather than judging me when I came out with my gifts, they have embraced them and encouraged me every step of the way. I know that I have made them proud.

Mom took care of me. She got me out of bed every morning. She hugged me while I screamed in pain, fed me, bathed me, and stayed with me at the hospital for days on end. She was always by my side and was an angel through it all. She only showed me love and support, and she always put me first. I couldn't have done it without her. I'm so blessed to have her as my mother.

Dad is a busy man, but despite running his own business, he would still drop everything to take me to the best doctors. If I ever needed him, day or night, all I had to do was call. He was always so strong and positive. He didn't just believe I would get better, he *knew* it. He is the wisest and most genuine person I've ever met. He may have started off as a skeptic, but now he is my number one fan, and he loves telling everyone that his daughter is a medium. He always believed I could do anything I put my mind to. He inspires me, and I'll always look up to him.

These past six years, Chip has been my therapist, my friend, my healer. He made me laugh when I needed levity, and he never left my side. Not only did he lie with me all day when I was bedridden, but when I started walking again, he was there as I took those baby steps in the backyard. He was with me every step of the way. Every time I had surgery, he knew exactly what I needed. He's my son, and I'm so grateful to him.

Without God and Spirit, there would be no me, and there would be no book. Learning to trust and have faith, learning to surrender has been a crucial part of the healing process and the spiritual journey that has led me here. Believing that God has a bigger plan, I've learned that my purpose here is much bigger than I ever imagined. They have shown me miracles exist, and that anything is possible. They helped me believe again and see there are greater things to live for. They helped me give someone else a second chance and save a life. They taught me to love myself, trust myself, have faith in my gifts, and share my healing with others. Thank you for helping me find the missing piece to the puzzle. Thank you for all the blessings and everyone I get to meet here and in spirit.

My grandma Luisa—I inherited not only her name, but also her gifts. She has been guiding me and supporting me from the other side since she passed in March 2008, and her loving presence was often a much-needed balm on my soul when I was suffering.

I'd also like to thank Dr. Alexandre Demoura and New York University Hospital-Spine Center. When all the other doctors gave me false hope, he looked at my scans and came up with a clear plan. He genuinely wanted to help me, and he did. He gave me a second chance at life, and I will forever be grateful.

Thanks to Dr. Jerzy Macura with Long Island Jewish Hospital, who operated on me for SMA syndrome. He was compassionate, kind, and he also saved my life. He operated just in time.

Thanks to Dr. Joseph Del Pizzo and New York Presbyterian, who cured my Nutcracker Syndrome by donating my kidney. He did something that had never been done before, and he also gave me another chance at life. Thanks also to Marian Charlton, my transplant coordinator, for helping me through that process and making it all go smoothly.

Thanks to the New York Spine Institute, where I went to rehab/physical therapy for over five years. They were patient, taught me to work hard, and gave me the tools I needed to learn to function again and again and again.

Thanks to Dr. Michelle Pfeffer, my chiropractor/massage therapist of five years. She has helped me with my pain and range of motion, and I'm grateful for her enormous heart.

Thanks to Winter Brook, my mentor and friend. She has had my back since we met. She supports me, encourages me, teaches me, and inspires me. We have shared some amazing spiritual experiences, and she has pushed me in so many ways that have helped me grow. She believes in me and wants me to succeed. I'm so grateful I can count on her. She is my cheerleader, and I am hers.

Thanks to my in-laws, Bob and Kathy, for the rides, the meals, and being there when we needed them most. Most of all, I thank them for raising such an incredible son.

Thanks to all my family and friends for being there on my hardest days. I know it was not easy to see me like that, but you all pushed me and helped me in some way. Thank you for checking in, making sure Billy was okay, stopping by, calling, sending a card, bringing a home-cooked meal, whatever it was I needed. Thank you for believing in me when I could not believe in myself. Thank you for replacing my tears with laughter. And a very big thank you for all your healing prayers.

Thanks to my amazing clients and supporters for trusting me with their hearts and souls and loved ones in spirit.

Thanks to my co-writer and friend, Cristina Moracho, for helping me share my story, and for being so sensitive and compassionate with some of the more delicate topics. I feel like we've known each other a long time. You made me feel comfortable and really supported me through some of the hardest memories. You walked me through it, and it was truly healing. We had some good laughs, too! I am excited to close this chapter and start a new one. I know there will be a part two!

French Country Sofa
Jessica Zerniko / Sept 18 2018 / Living Sofas & Loveseat

Italia appt - apt local